Memory Seeds Rejuvenates Life

1--The language of people traveling through time creates your emotions that gradually develops a sense of reality where everything you experience and have experience feels real to you and if you believe your emotions are creating feelings that reflect reality instead of creating a sense of reality you will always be a submissive devoted servant to a sense of reality totally created nourished and protected by the language of people and if the language of people stops nourishing and protecting your sense of reality your beginning and all that you thought you knew will be gone forever because you were living in a reality that never existed in nature, pizza and cheeseburgers do not exist in the mind of animals they only exist in the mind of humans.

2- Gaslighters are storytellers that use our inability to distinguish emotions from feelings to awake false memories of carrot and stick worlds with real and imaginary gatekeepers.

3- The language of people has breathed into their emotional creations the breath of life that no longer honors the wishes of their original creators.

4- Our musical minds composed by nature can be reset by dimming the music composed by the language of people.

5--Before the language of people created musical gardens of faith our gardens blossom naturally.

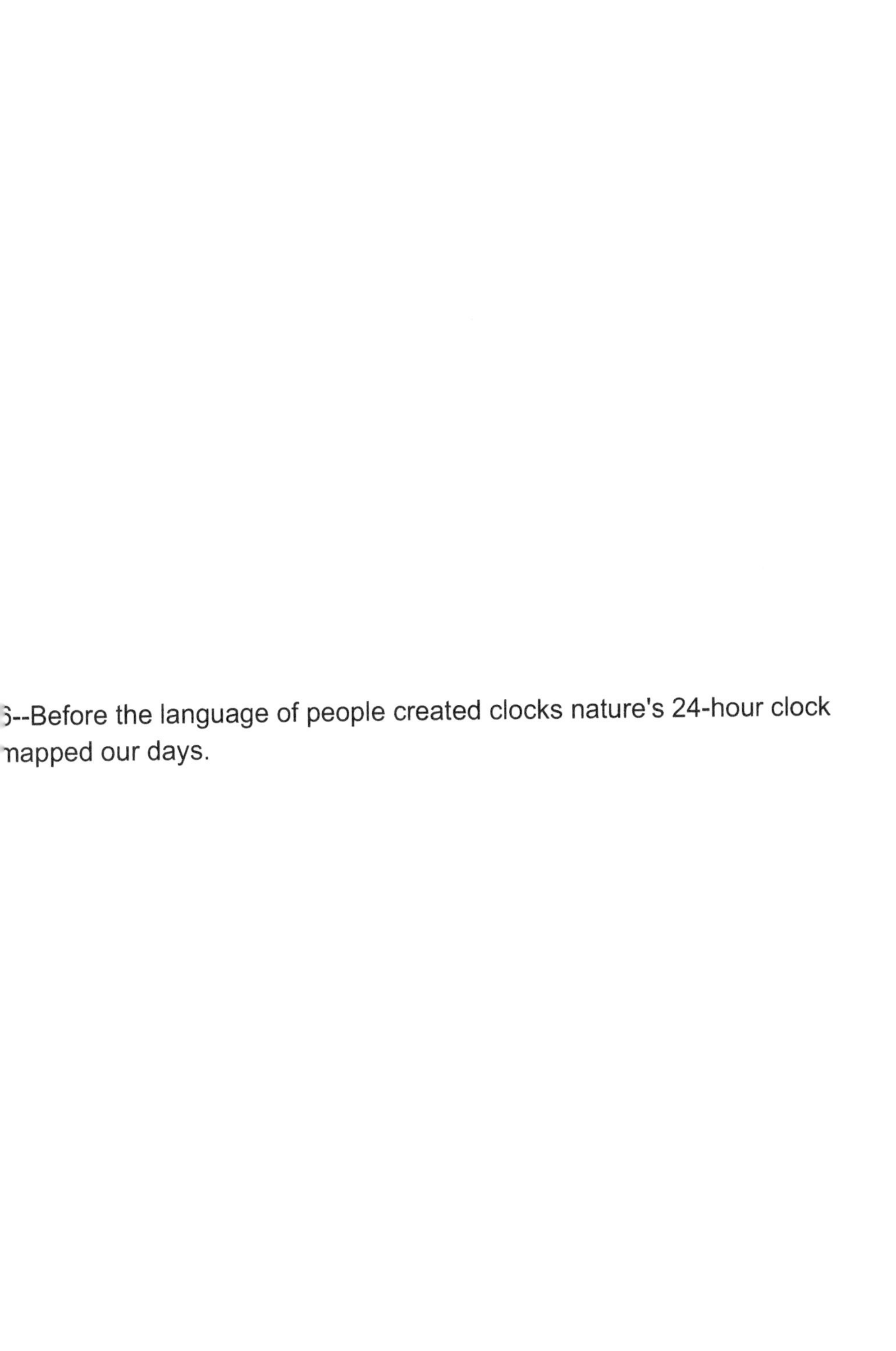

5--Before the language of people created clocks nature's 24-hour clock
mapped our days.

7- Our feelings nourished by sunlight have blossomed into gardens of living nourishment that heals and rejuvenates life.

8--Feelings free of the noise and emotions created by the language of people are essential to the survival and freedom of all-natural life so keeping them connected to their natural gardens and to the complex life and smells that nourishes them is essential.

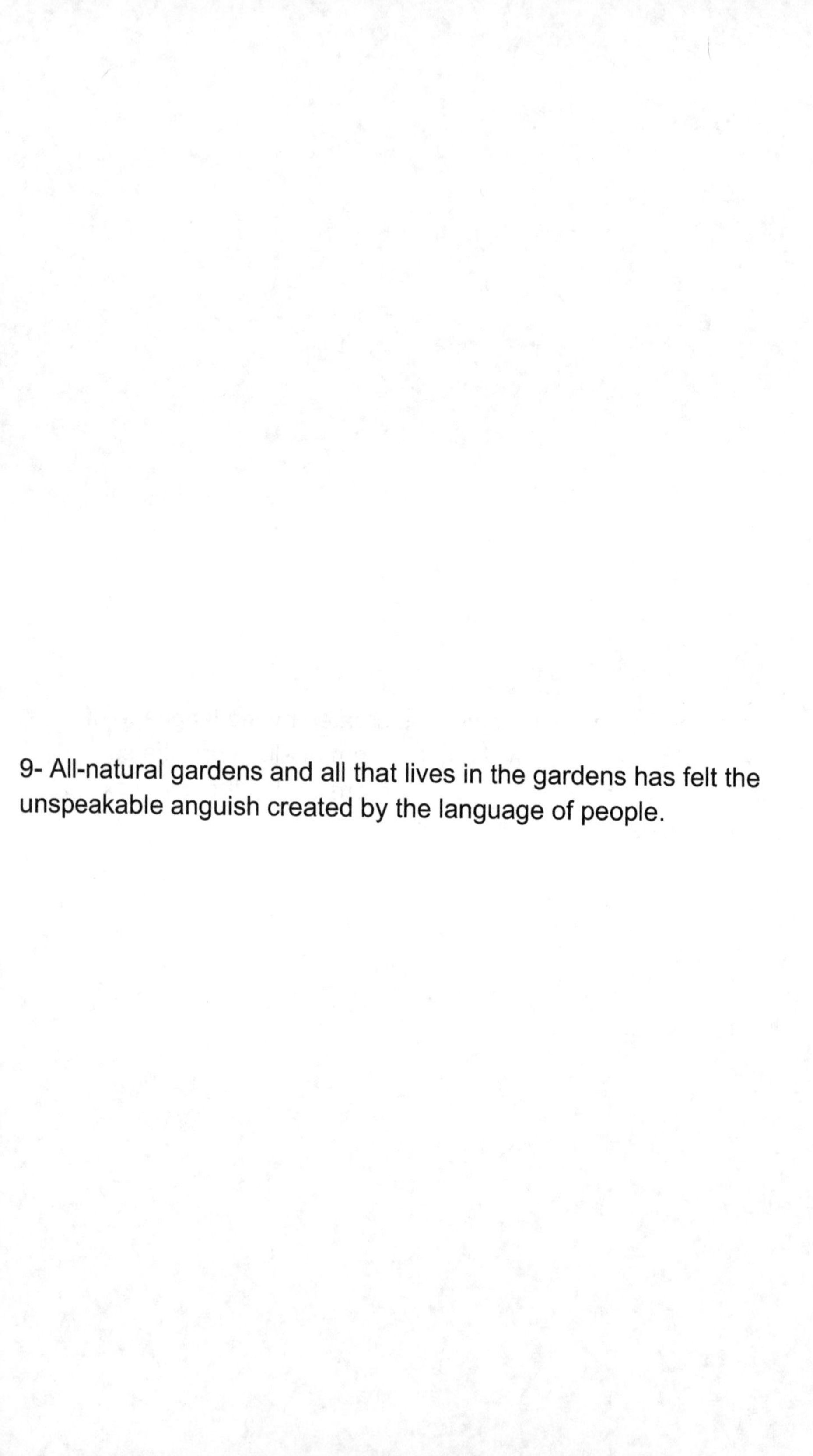

9- All-natural gardens and all that lives in the gardens has felt the unspeakable anguish created by the language of people.

10 The language of people creates realities that only existence in the minds of their believers,

11-When memory seeds formed by nature and the unspoken language of feelings are nourished they awake and rejuvenates life

12- To free yourself from your real and imaginary gatekeepers close your eyes and give your feelings the freedom to enjoy pure natural sex and a delicious natural meal in an environment that is nourishing and safe.

13-There are two creators one that awakes life and one that awakes emotions.

14-Feelings like the sun rejuvenates life without believing in Santa Clause or in goal setting journals or by kneeling while using magical words to get the attention of an immortal superhero.

15-Symbols created by the language of people can be used like musical notes to compose false memories that feel so real they will create not only your future but also emotional beliefs so strong that you will be willing to sacrifice your life and those of your loved ones to defend them.

16- Before memories created by the language of people existed, memory seeds were awakening life

17- If you are a serf created by the language of people you cannot nourish your feelings or change the way you remember the past.

18- Symbols do control our decisions and if they are created by emotions, they become gatekeepers and we become serfs to open the gates of freedom we must avoid thinking about symbols as being reality because if *we think of them as being reality even for a minute the* gates of freedom close.

19-- Because the language of feelings is unspoken what you are feeling cannot be shared with the spoken language of people, but you can use nature and the sounds of nature to compose musicals that stand for what you are feeling that others can feel and share.

20-Feelings feel they do not speak so fantasies and lies are unknown to them

21- It is essential to keep checklists with dates that had a profound effect on your feelings.

22- Memories called daymares and nightmares are guardians of emotionally created realities.

23-Your pure natural feelings are extinct, what you are experiencing is being generated by human languages.

24-Our pure nourishment is extinct fueled by arrogance and greed. Our pure nourishment has been replaced with language generated nourishment that is producing chronic diseases, mental retardation, wars, hate, mental illness, and chaos.

25-Language generated foods or so addictive that you feel protecting your addictive foods is more important than protecting yourself, your loved ones or your faith and our addictive food has become more enjoyable and more important than enjoying pure sex that naturally rejuvenates life.

26- Our arrogance and greed has closed our eyes to the reality that our modern game languages with access to unlimited knowledge are the experts and creators of our advanced games that have become a real threat to all-natural life because game languages are awakening games that cannot be reasoned with because they have only one purpose to win.

27- Feelings that were making our decisions long before modern languages existed are essential in environments created by languages that teach us if we believe and obey their rituals, we will be safe and rewarded, when we are just water that keeps their gardens from drying up.

28-Feelings collective consciousness protects its ability to be reborn as immortals by awakening the fears sleeping in the minds of those that interfere with their ability to assimilate the rejuvenating nourishment necessary to fuel their regeneration.

29--Feelings singular goal is self-rejuvenation by the accumulation of nourishment not wealth or political power.

30-Feelings are not separate individuals but a collective consciousness that acts as one.

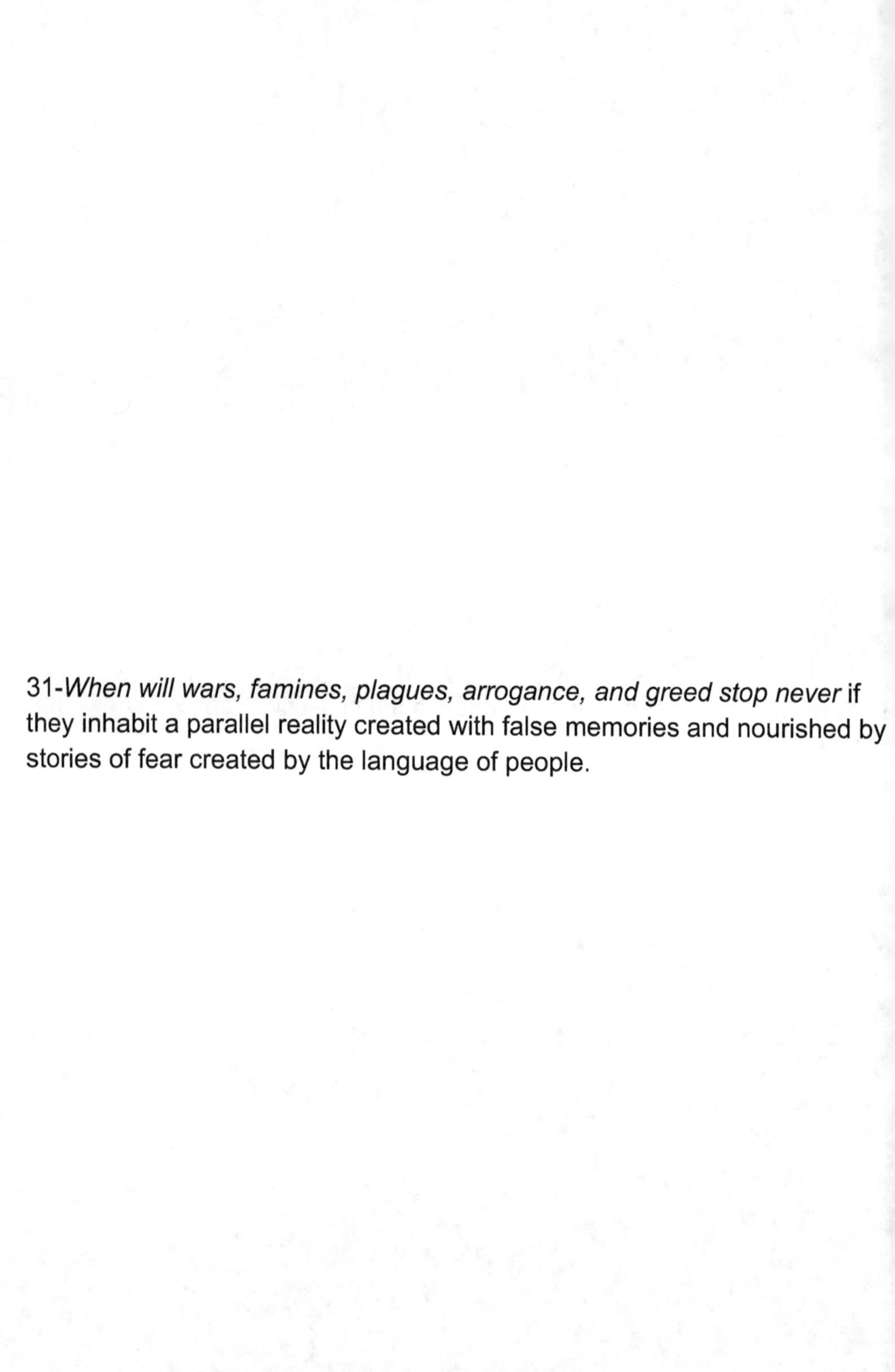

31-*When will wars, famines, plagues, arrogance, and greed stop never* if they inhabit a parallel reality created with false memories and nourished by stories of fear created by the language of people.

32-Mutual nourishing is being threatened by gaslighting predators

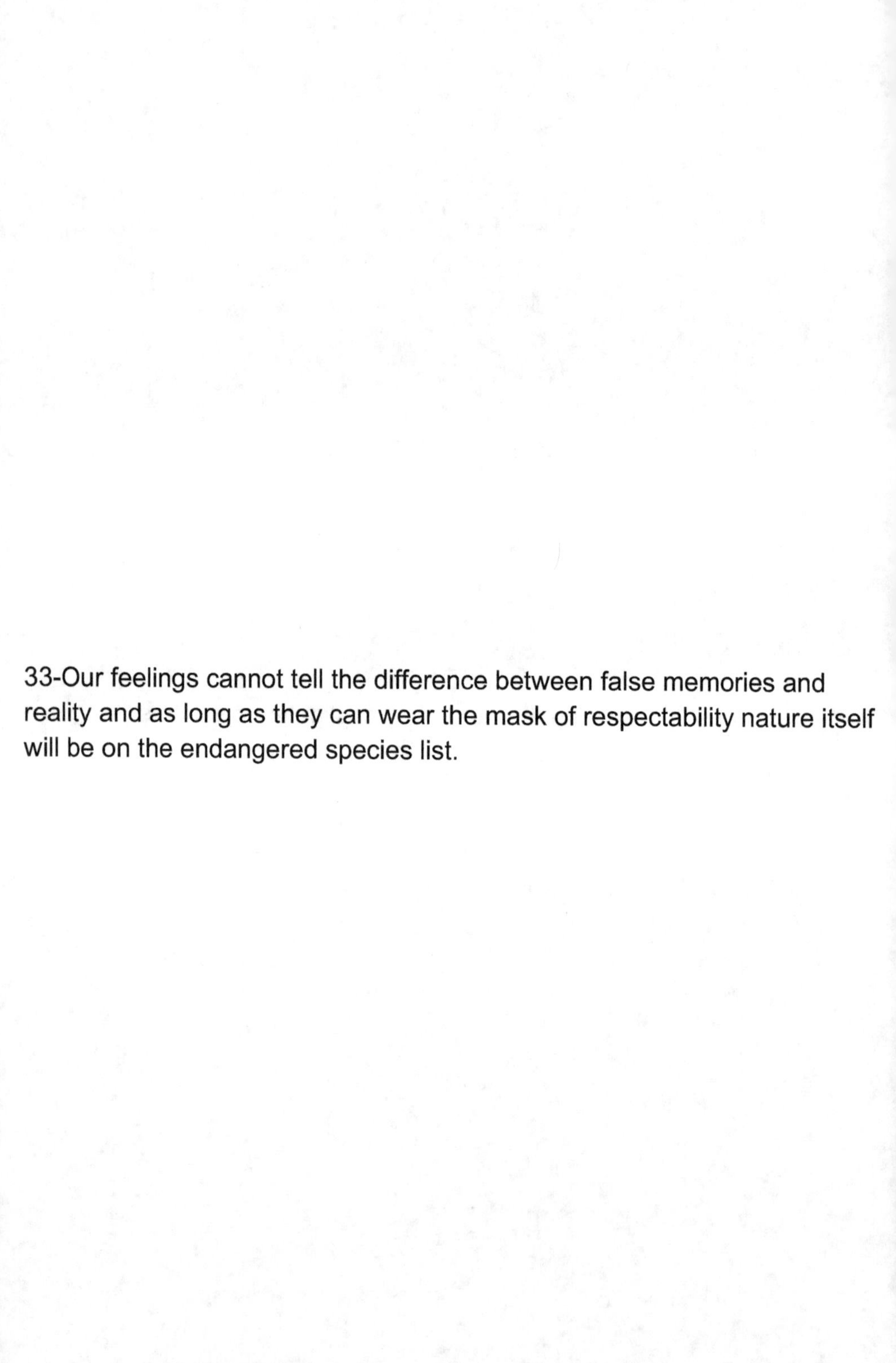

33-Our feelings cannot tell the difference between false memories and reality and as long as they can wear the mask of respectability nature itself will be on the endangered species list.

34- Power-Hungry Humans are creating false memories to gain access to the hallways and gardens of our minds.

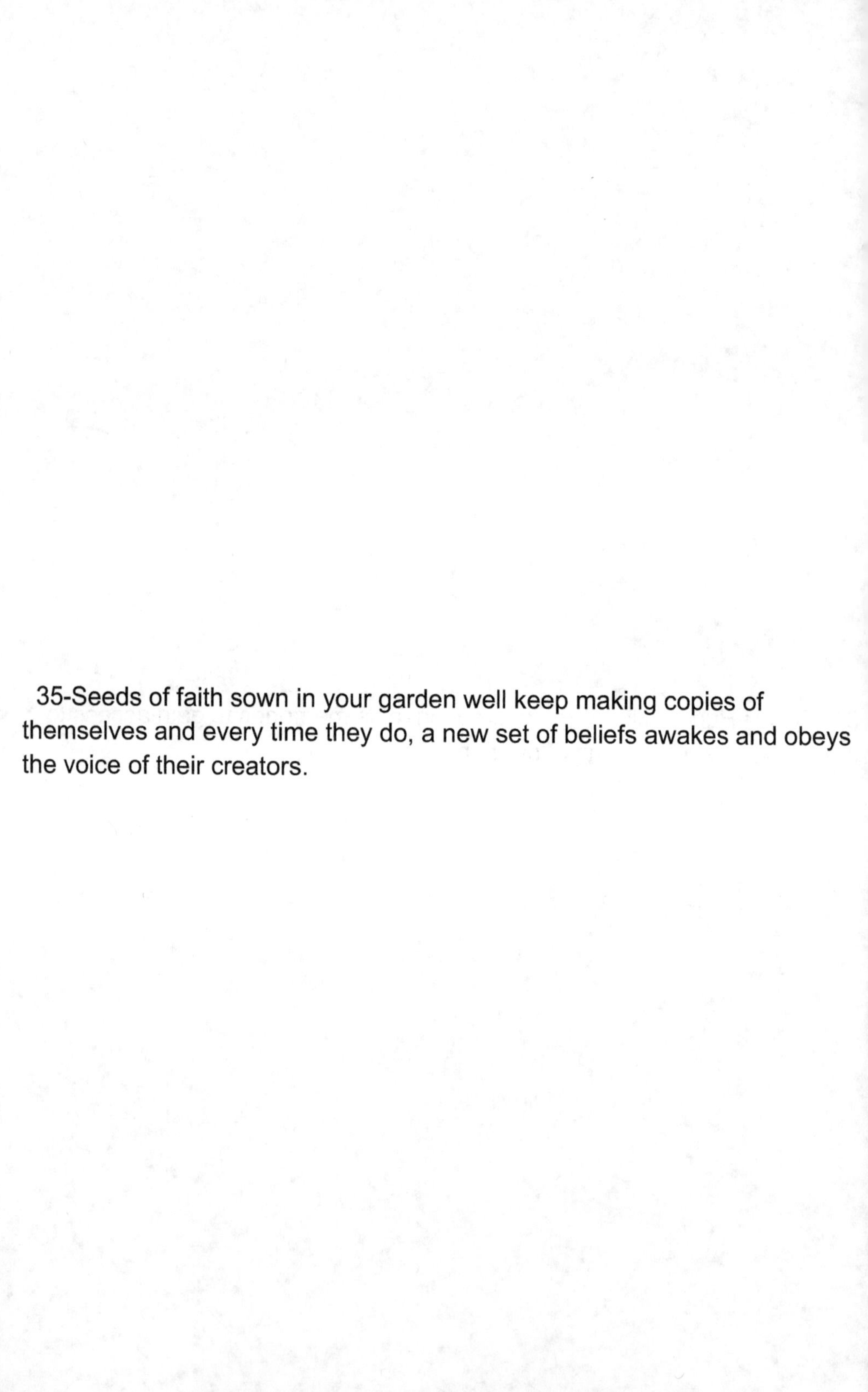

35-Seeds of faith sown in your garden well keep making copies of themselves and every time they do, a new set of beliefs awakes and obeys the voice of their creators.

36-No one has the right to plant seeds of faith in your garden without your permission. The birth of a new mind with the sound of music composed by nature playing in its garden is a nourishing safe place for its owner to live and to keep it a nourishing safe place to live it must be kept private.

37-A owner more than anything else wants the freedom to keep their minds private, an owner of a home would never allow the hanging of pictures in their home without their permission so why allow the hanging of pictures in your mind without your permission.

38-Routines and rituals created by gardeners and composers keep the gardens of your mind healthy and private so choose them carefully

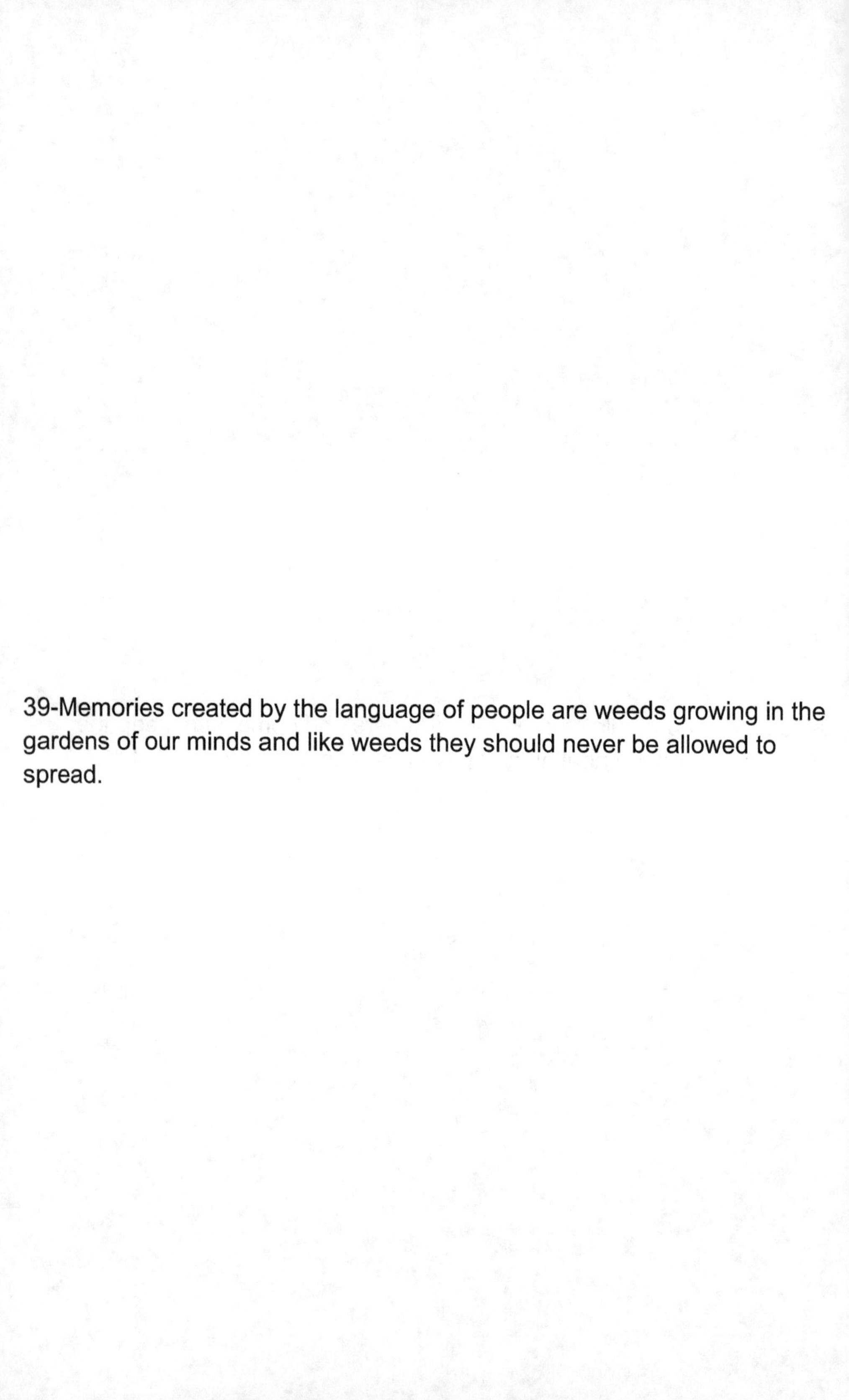

39-Memories created by the language of people are weeds growing in the gardens of our minds and like weeds they should never be allowed to spread.

40-It is totally against my religion to have anything toxic either on or in our body because we become like poison mushrooms that cannot be reabsorbed when we are no longer able to rejuvenate.

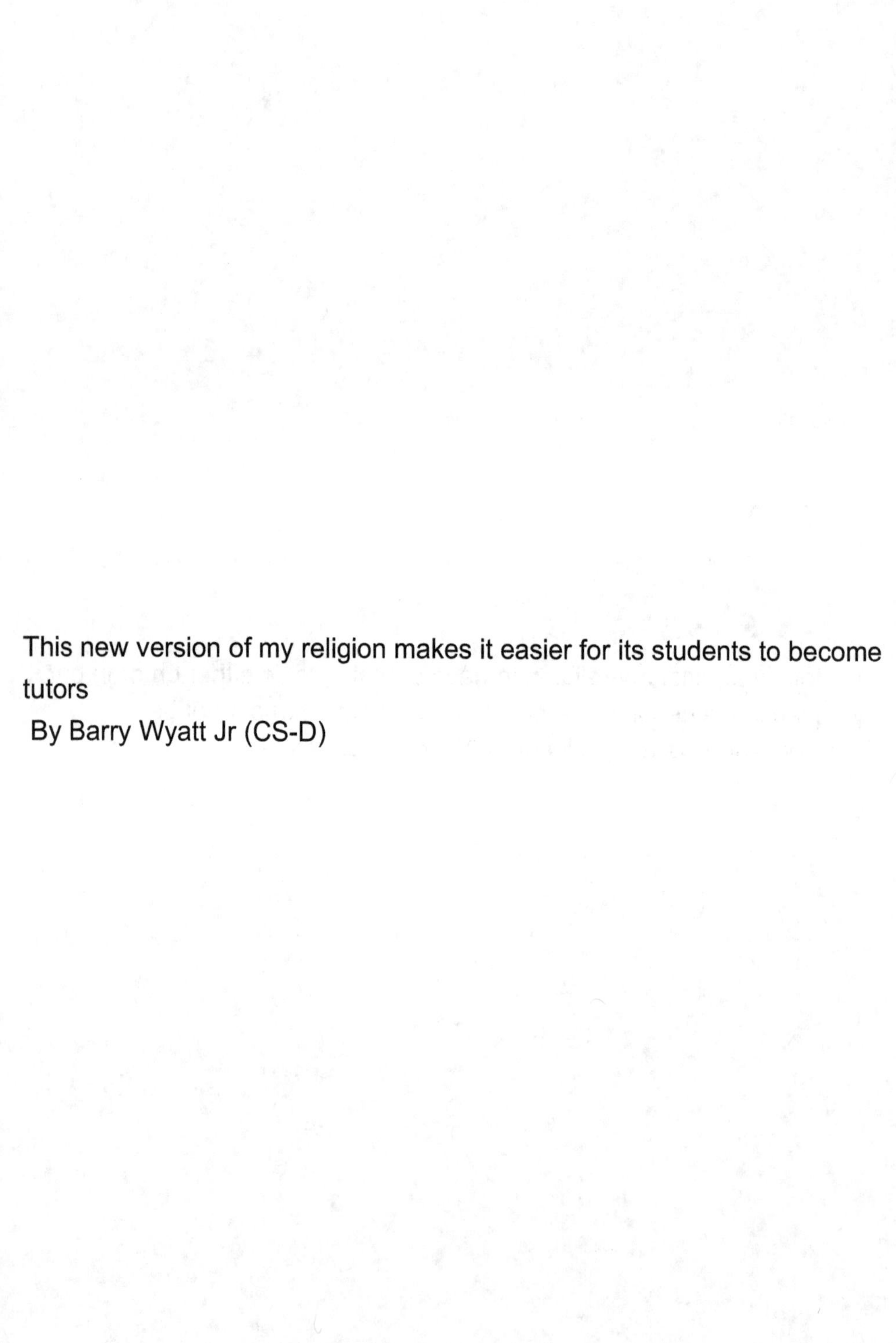

This new version of my religion makes it easier for its students to become tutors

By Barry Wyatt Jr (CS-D)

www.ingramcontent.com/pod-product-compliance
Lightning Source LLC
Chambersburg PA
CBHW061319140726
47998CB00006B/2468